Martin Luther King, Jr.

Kitson Jazynka

NATIONAL
GEOGRAPHIC

Washington, D.C.

To bright young readers everywhere,
especially Max & Quinn —K. J.

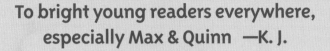

The publisher and author gratefully acknowledge the review of proofs for this book by historian
Michael K. Honey.

Library of Congress Cataloging-in-Publication Data
Jazynka, Kitson.
Martin Luther King, Jr. / by Kitson Jazynka.
p. cm. Includes index.
ISBN 978-1-4263-1087-4 (pbk. : alk. paper) -- ISBN 978-1-4263-1088-1 (library binding : alk. paper)
1. King, Martin Luther, Jr., 1929-1968--Juvenile literature. 2. African Americans--Biography--Juvenile
literature. 3. Civil rights workers--United States--Biography--Juvenile literature. 4. Baptists--United
States--Clergy--Biography--Juvenile literature. 5. African Americans--Civil rights--History--20th
century--Juvenile literature. I. Title.
E185.97.K5J377 2012
323.092--dc23
[B]
2012034595

Printed in the United States of America
12/WOR/1

Table of Contents

Who Was Martin Luther King, Jr.?

Can you imagine a world where laws kept black and white people apart? Where black children couldn't swim in the same pools as white children? Or go to the same schools? A place where laws made it hard for black people to vote? Or where a black person had to stand up on a bus so a white person could sit down?

This world was real. And it happened in the United States.

Words to Know

CIVIL RIGHTS: The rights that all people in the U.S. have to be treated as equals

Statues at the National Civil Rights Museum in Memphis, Tennessee

Martin Luther King, Jr., worked hard to change rules so they would be the same for whites and blacks. He didn't do it by fighting. He helped change unfair laws by making people think. He did it by making people feel. He did it with his words.

Words to Know

PROTEST: To say you don't agree with something

Protesters

People who protest are called protesters. When protesters want unfair things changed, they sometimes march to show others that they do not agree with what is happening.

Dr. King marches in a protest.

Lots of black people and white people helped Dr. King protest those laws. This made many people angry because they didn't want change. But in the end, the protesters won. And the rules changed forever.

Growing Up

Dr. King was born in 1929 in Atlanta, Georgia. He was named after his father. He was called M.L.

Small but strong, M.L. rode bikes with his brother and sister.

That's a Fact! M.L.'s boyhood home on Auburn Avenue in Atlanta is open to the public.

The boyhood home of Martin Luther King, Jr.

Tours of the Birth Home Begin Every Half-Hour At Visitor Information Station ←522 Auburn Ave. N.E.

Birth Home Of Martin L. King, Jr.

M.L.'s father was a minister at Ebenezer Baptist Church in Atlanta, Georgia.

M.L.'s father was the minister of a church. He taught his children to stand up for what is right. He taught them to speak out against what is wrong. He taught them that all people deserve justice, which means that they should be treated fairly.

When he was six, M.L.'s best friend told him he was no longer allowed to play with M.L. Why? Because M.L. was black and his friend was white.

Segregation (SEG-rih-GAY-shun) laws were meant to keep black people and white people apart. They kept kids apart, too. M.L. felt bad. Why wasn't he good enough to play with his friend?

Words to Know

SEGREGATION: Keeping someone or something apart from others

This movie theater had a separate rear entrance for blacks.

M.L.'s mother told him he was just as good as anybody else. And she told him the world was wrong. He wiped his tears. Then M.L. promised that one day he would change the world.

Mother

Father

Grandmother

M.L.

Brother Alfred Daniel

Sister Christine

M.L.'s family

Change for Peace

Martin Luther King, Jr., received the Nobel Peace Prize in 1964. At that time, he was the youngest person ever to have received it. He was just 35 years old.

Nobel Peace Prize medal

Words to Know

NOBEL PEACE PRIZE: An important award given for outstanding work toward peace

In His Time

Martin Luther King, Jr., was a boy in the late 1930s. Many things were different from how they are today.

Transportation

Most people still traveled by horse and buggy. Only some people were lucky enough to have cars.

Cities

Some of New York City's famous skyscrapers were finished in the 1930s. Two of them are the Empire State Building (left) and Rockefeller Center.

Money

Candy bars cost about a penny. That doesn't sound like much, but dollars and pennies were worth a lot more back then.

U.S. Events

Many people did not have jobs during this time, called the Great Depression. Most people had very little money.

Toys and Free Time

Children played board games and listened to programs on the radio for fun.

School

Times were tough. Some families couldn't afford to send their kids to school. Books, clothes, and shoes were too expensive.

A Way With Words

M.L. grew up listening to sermons in church. He learned how powerful words can be used to help people understand ideas.

When M.L. was 14, he entered a speech contest. He put his anger about the unfairness of separate rules for white people and black people into words. He made people think. He made them feel. The judges loved his speech, and he won.

In His Own Words

". . . let us see to it that . . . we give fair play and free opportunity for all people."

—from M.L.'s winning speech when he was 14 years old.

Ebenezer Baptist Church is where M.L. learned the power of words.

That's a Fact!

M.L. not only grew up in Ebenezer Baptist Church, but he later became a minister there as well.

Words to Know

SERMON: A long talk, usually given in church

White passengers could sit in the front of the bus.
Black passengers had to sit in the back or stand.

On the bus ride home from the speech contest, the driver told M.L. and his teacher to give up their seats to white people. M.L. had to stand for two hours. He was mad. But he didn't say anything. He knew he could be arrested, hurt, or even killed if he did.

NOTICE

IT IS REQUIRED BY LAW. UNDER PENALTY OF FINE OF $5.00 TO $25.00. THAT WHITE AND NEGRO PASSENGERS MUST OCCUPY THE RESPECTIVE SPACE OR SEATS INDICATED BY SIGNS IN THIS VEHICLE.

TEXAS PENAL CODE: ARTICLE 1659. SEC.4
DALLAS CITY ORDINANCE: NO. 2904

A man attaches a segregated seating sign to a bus in the southern U.S.

A Student of Peace

M.L. (third from the left) with fellow students at Morehouse College

That's a Fact! M.L. skipped two grades in high school. He started college very early—at age 15.

M.L. worked hard in school. He finished college when he was 19 years old. He moved to the northeastern U.S. and continued in school. He wanted to be a minister like his father.

Morehouse College

In 1952, M.L. met Coretta Scott and fell in love. They got married and moved south to Alabama. There, M.L. worked as a minister. By 1955, he had gone as far as you can go in school. He had earned the title "doctor." Now he was "Dr. King."

Dexter Avenue Baptist Church in Montgomery, Alabama, where Dr. King was minister

Dr. Martin Luther King, Jr., and Coretta Scott King in 1956

Helping Others

A white man and a black man drink at separate drinking fountains.

The Kings moved back to the South to work for equal rights. They saw that not much had changed for black people there. They still couldn't swim in pools or go to school with whites. They still had to stand on buses so white people could sit.

In Alabama, Dr. King had a chance to help. A bus driver told a woman named Rosa Parks to give up her seat to a white person. But she didn't get up. Rosa Parks was arrested because she had broken the law.

Rosa Parks

The bus stop where Rosa Parks waited in 1955

Lots of people went to a meeting to decide what to do. Maids, janitors, and other working people rode the buses. They asked people not to ride buses until blacks and whites had the same rules. They called it a boycott. They put Dr. King in charge because he had a way with words.

In His Own Words

"Always feel that you count. Always feel that you have worth . . ."

Words to Know

BOYCOTT: To stop using a service as a way to protest it

For more than a year, black people walked. They took cabs. They even rode mules to get around. The boycott was not easy. But finally, people listened. Black people and white people would have the same rules on buses. Unfortunately, many white people did not follow the new rules.

People boycotting the buses wave to an empty bus driving by.

Dr. King and Coretta Scott King lead a five-day march to Montgomery, Alabama, in 1965.

In His Own Words

"Injustice anywhere is a threat to justice everywhere."

Dr. King went all over the country giving speeches. He talked about injustice and civil rights. He made people think. He made people feel. And he asked people to join him in protests for change.

Blacks and whites marched together to protest bad laws. They went to places where only whites were allowed. A lot of them got arrested. Angry people called them names. Sometimes the marchers were hurt or even killed.

Words to Know

INJUSTICE: Behavior or treatment that is unfair

Newspapers, television, and radio reported it all. People around the country were mad. They saw how bad it was to have separate rules.

Peaceful Protests

Dr. King wanted to make the world a better place. He did this with peace, not hate or violence.

People sometimes hurt him. But Dr. King did not hurt them back. He fought back with peaceful protests and powerful words.

In His Own Words

". . . love is the most durable power in the world."

One person who saw what was going on was President John F. Kennedy. The President wanted to show that he agreed that rules should be the same for blacks and whites. So he invited Dr. King to visit him at the White House.

Words to Know

PEACEFUL: Quiet and not disturbed by fighting or arguing

VIOLENCE: Hurting someone or something

Dr. King

President Kennedy

President John F. Kennedy met with Dr. King and other civil rights leaders at the White House.

8 Awesome Facts About Dr. King

1

Dr. King and his father were both named Michael King. But his father changed their names in 1934.

2

Once Dr. King was hit with a brick during a peaceful march. He didn't fight back. He kept walking.

3

Dr. King liked to dance.

4

Dr. King learned good ideas from a man from India named Gandhi (GHAN-dee). He used peaceful protest to fight unfair laws.

5 Dr. King gave 2,500 speeches during the last 11 years of his life.

6 The statue of Dr. King at his memorial in Washington, D.C., is huge. Its head weighs 27 tons.

7 Dr. King told people to love each other like brothers and sisters.

8 Dr. King and Coretta Scott King had four children: Yolanda, Martin Luther III, Dexter, and Bernice.

Dr. King's Dream

That's a Fact!

A draft of Dr. King's "I Have a Dream" speech is still located at Morehouse College.

Thousands of people gathered for the March on Washington in 1963.

It was August 28, 1963, in Washington, D.C. In the same city where our country makes its laws, a huge crowd of people—black and white—cheered. They had come to stand with Dr. King and protest bad laws. Everyone in the crowd wanted the same rules for white people and black people.

Dr. King's voice boomed as he gave his most famous speech, called "I Have a Dream." Dr. King's dream was for all people to be treated the same.

Hard Times

Three months after Dr. King's speech, President Kennedy was assassinated. It was a hard time for the United States. But the next President, Lyndon Johnson, kept working to change the rules.

President Johnson and Dr. King shaking hands

Words to Know

ASSASSINATE: To murder an important person

In His Own Words

"I have a dream that my four little children will one day live in a nation where they will not be judged by the color of their skin, but by the content of their character."

Dr. King speaks at the Lincoln Memorial.

His Final Years

The rules did change in 1964 and again in 1965. Laws were now the same for black people and white people. But not everyone followed the new rules right away. For the next several years, Dr. King and many others kept working. Dr. King gave speeches. He planned peaceful protests. He helped others.

In 1966, Dr. King walked black children to Mississippi schools that used to be all-white.

In 1968, Dr. King was in Memphis, Tennessee. He was helping black garbage collectors protest for better pay. But angry people still did not want change. A man with a gun assassinated Dr. King.

Black and white people around the world were very sad. They had lost a man who made them think and feel. They had lost a man who helped make our world a better place with peace and justice. But Dr. King left us his words to remember him by.

1929
Born in Atlanta, Georgia, on January 15

1948
Graduates from college; becomes a minister

1952
Met Coretta Scott. They were married a year later.

1954
Starts work at Dexter Avenue Baptist Church in Montgomery Alabama

Dr. King's dream lives on today.

★ ★

1962

Visits the
White House

1963

Arrested at a
peaceful protest
and jailed for
two weeks

1963

Speaks at
the March on
Washington

A Memorial to Peace

You can visit a national memorial to Dr. King. It is in Washington, D.C. There you can read his words about his hope that people could live together peacefully and with justice. You can also stand next to a 30-foot statue of him. It is called the "Stone of Hope."

From far away, the "Stone of Hope" looks gray. But up close, it is really many colors. The colors stand for all the different people in the world. That's because Dr. King stood up for our right to all be treated fairly.

★ ★ ★ ★ ★ ★ ★ ★ ★ ★ ★ ★ ★ ★ ★ ★ ★ ★ ★ ★

1964
Arrested and jailed for demanding to eat at a white-only restaurant

1964
Awarded the Nobel Peace Prize

1965
Leads 25,000 people in a march to protest unfair voting laws

The "Stone of Hope" is carved out of granite. This color rock is called "Shrimp Pink."

Words to Know

MEMORIAL: Something created to remind people of a person, event, or important idea

1968

Killed on April 4 in Memphis, Tennessee

1983

A new national holiday honors Dr. King on his birthday.

2011

National memorial to Dr. King in Washington, D.C., opens.

Be a Quiz Whiz!

See how many questions you can get right! **Answers are at the bottom of page 45.**

Dr. King won a speech contest when he was:
A. 14
B. 18
C. 24
D. 9

Dr. King gave his "I Have a Dream" speech in:
A. Atlanta, Georgia
B. Washington, D.C.
C. Memphis, Tennessee
D. Boston, Massachusetts

When he was 19, Martin Luther King, Jr.:
A. Started college
B. Graduated from college
C. Got married
D. Moved to Montgomery, Alabama

4

When he was a child, Dr. King could no longer play with his best friend because:

A. He was black and his friend was white
B. He wouldn't share
C. He was poor
D. He played too rough

5

Dr. King's family nicknamed him:

A. Marty
B. Smarty
C. M.L.
D. Doc

6

The day he was killed, Dr. King was in Memphis, Tennessee, to:

A. Visit family
B. Help garbage collectors
C. Sightsee
D. Teach

7

The "Stone of Hope" is carved from granite called:

A. Dark Gray
B. Peaches-n-Cream
C. Kingstone
D. Shrimp Pink

Answers: 1) A, 2) B, 3) B, 4) A, 5) C, 6) B, 7) D

Glossary

ASSASSINATE: To murder an important person

INJUSTICE: Behavior or treatment that is unfair

MEMORIAL: Something created to remind people of a person, event, or important idea

PROTEST: To say you don't agree with something

SERMON: A long talk, usually given in church

BOYCOTT: To stop using a service as a way to protest it

CIVIL RIGHTS: The rights that all people in the U.S. have to be treated as equals

NOBEL PEACE PRIZE: An important award given for outstanding work toward peace

PEACEFUL: Quiet and not disturbed by fighting or arguing

SEGREGATION: Keeping someone or something apart from others

VIOLENCE: Hurting someone or something

Index

Bold page numbers indicate illustrations.